THE FOUNDATIONS OF WISDOM

VOLUME 1

LOGIC STUDY GUIDE

THE FOUNDATIONS OF WISDOM

VOLUME 1

LOGIC STUDY GUIDE

FR. SEBASTIAN WALSHE, O. PRAEM.

TAN Books
Gastonia, North Carolina

Cover design by Andrew Schmalen

ISBN: 978-1-5051-2637-2

Published in the United States by

TAN Books
PO Box 269
Gastonia, NC 28053

www.TANBooks.com

CONTENTS

Introduction 1

List of Important Definitions for Logic 4

Chapter 1. 6

Chapter 2. 8

Chapter 3. 10

Chapter 4. 13

Chapter 5. 15

Chapter 6. 17

Chapter 7. 19

Chapter 8. 24

Chapter 9. 28

Chapter 10 31

Final Essay Question. 34

Introduction

This is a study guide to accompany volume 1 of *The Foundations of Wisdom: Logic*. In this study guide, I will explain the overall structure of volume 1 and how to read the text of volume 1. I will also include essential chapter-by-chapter questions you should be asking and answering as you read through the text. Finally, I will include exercises to assist you in practicing and using the tools you should have acquired while reading this text.

The Need for a Teacher

The first thing you should know about how to read this book is that you need a teacher to read it well. No book, no matter how well-written, is sufficient as a guide for the life of the mind. This is even truer in the case of matters which are difficult to learn. The reason for this is obvious: you can't ask a book questions (and if you do, don't expect the book to answer!). The number of potential questions which may arise in the mind of a student is practically limitless, and no book can anticipate all of them, and even if it did, the book would be so cumbersome and large that it would be useless as a tool for teaching. A good teacher will be able to answer many, if not all, of the questions any given student might ask about the content of the book.

Secondly, a teacher is one who knows what the student does not, and therefore, the teacher can do what no book can do: he can propose new words to express the same concepts. If a student finds certain words or statements in this book to be unfamiliar or obscure, a teacher who knows what the book is asserting can propose alternative words which are more familiar to the student and easier for him to understand.

Finally, every book written about any subject matter presupposes that a student already knows certain truths and has certain experiences. For example, a book on biology presupposes that the student has experience with living things such as plants and animals. Logic is no different. But it may happen that a student is lacking one or more of the basic experiences or foundational truths presupposed by this book. In that case, a teacher can help supply the missing elements in the student's formation (for example, by giving reasons for the truths presupposed to what is asserted in the book).

For these reasons, as well as some others, I strongly recommend that in addition to reading the *Logic* book and this accompanying study guide, try to find someone who already knows this subject matter well who can fulfill the role of a teacher.

The Overall Plan of the Logic Book

Logic is an art. When we say logic is an art, we don't mean one of the fine arts like painting or sculpture. That is the sense of the word "art" most familiar to modern students. Instead, when we say that logic is an art, we mean a kind of correct or right knowledge about things to be made. In this sense, any practical knowledge about things to be made can be called an art. Farming, carpentry, architecture, boat-making, and medicine are all examples of art in this broader sense. Taken in this sense, every art aims at some good. Farming aims at producing an abundance of nutritious food; architecture aims at producing safe and beautiful buildings for shelter; medicine aims at producing health, and so on.

Logic also aims at some good: truth.

And just as every art produces tools to more easily acquire the good it aims at, so too does logic. The art of agriculture makes tools like plows and sprinklers to more effectively grow an abundance of food. The art of carpentry makes hammers and nails and saws to more effectively produce wooden items like chairs and beds. The art of medicine makes and uses stethoscopes and medicines to more effectively produce health. Logic also makes tools for the mind to use in order to more effectively arrive at truth. These tools include definitions, statements, and arguments. Without these tools, we cannot reason well, especially about difficult matters.

Since the aim of this book is to give the reader some proficiency in the art of reasoning well, and since reasoning well requires that we can argue to true conclusions, this means that the student must be equipped to construct good arguments which conclude necessarily to true conclusions. Therefore, this book equips the student to make each step on the way to that end, and it also equips the student with the tools necessary to reason to truth.

The first six chapters of the book covers introductory principles such as the nature and purpose of philosophy in general and logic in particular. Chapter 7 considers the art of defining and teaches the student how to make and use the tool of definition; definitions are necessary since the meaning of the words in any given statement must be known before a judgment can be made about the truth of that statement. Chapter 8 considers the art of constructing true and necessary statements. These statements are also tools used by reason since they are required to express truth and also as premises for a good argument. Chapters 9 and 10 teach the student how to make and use the tool called argument, and especially syllogisms, which are the best kind of argument. Chapter 9 considers the valid forms of a syllogism and distinguishes them from invalid forms, since even true and necessary premises will only conclude to a true and necessary conclusion if the form of the argument is valid. Finally, chapter 10 teaches the student how to assemble the appropriate premises into a valid syllogism which concludes necessarily to a true statement (the conclusion). This kind of argument, called demonstration, is the most powerful tool of reason.

In summary, the overall plan of the book is as follows:

- Chapters 1-6: Principles of Philosophy and Logic
- Chapter 7: Making and using definitions
- Chapter 8: Making and using statements
- Chapters 9–10: Making and using arguments, especially syllogisms

Using Supplementary Texts

Some chapters refer the student to supplementary texts in the footnotes. These texts are, for the most part, original texts of great thinkers. Depending upon the abilities of the teacher and students, as well as upon the time you have to complete the course, these supplementary texts can be very helpful to examine a subject in greater detail. If the teacher is very knowledgeable and familiar with the supplementary text, and the students are more advanced, these texts will be very helpful for increasing the student's knowledge of logic. However, the course can be completed without reading the supplementary texts. They are options for those who desire to use them.

How Much Reading and Study Time Should Be Devoted to Each Part?

The time needed to cover the materials in this book is the sum of the time it takes to

1. read the book,
2. cover the material in class, and
3. do the exercises recommended by the book.

The amount of time it should take a student to read the book carefully is approximately five to ten hours. The amount of class time to cover the contents of this book should total to somewhere between fifty and sixty-five hours. Finally, the minimum amount of time needed to perform the recommended exercises in both the study guide and the book should be no less than twenty-five hours. So a student should expect that the total amount of time necessary to cover the entire contents of the *Logic* book with this accompanying study guide will be between eighty and one hundred hours.

As a ballpark figure, chapters 1-6 should take approximately twenty to twenty-five hours; chapter 7 should take approximately twenty to twenty-five hours; chapter 8 should take approximately five to ten hours; and chapters 9–10 should take approximately thirty-five to forty hours.

These are simply estimates based upon my experience teaching this material. There may be reasons or circumstances why a particular student might use significantly more time than what is recommended here, but it would be unusual that a student would need significantly less time than the seventy-five to ninety hours recommended here.

List of Important Definitions for Logic

The following definitions are important for understanding the *Logic* text. Because definitions are the seeds of all of our knowledge and are presupposed to everything else we can know, the student should memorize all of these definitions.

The best way to memorize these definitions is to sit down with a partner and verbally ask one another the definition of each term on this list. Once you can repeat the definitions three times quickly and without making a mistake, you can go on to the next one on the list until all of them are memorized. Some of these definitions pertain to the earlier chapters (like the definitions of philosophy and logic), while others pertain to the later chapters (such as the definition of demonstration).

Philosophy (ch. 2): An account of the ultimate causes of reality according to reason.

Truth (ch. 8): The conformance of the mind to reality.

Art (ch. 4): A fixed and definite method established by reason by which human acts reach their due ends by appropriate means.

Logic (ch. 4): The art of reasoning well. (nominal)
The art of habitually reasoning to true conclusions from true premises. (essential)

Speech (ch. 7): Vocal sound which signifies by convention.

Genus (ch. 7): A name used univocally, said of many things different in kind, signifying what they are.

Species (ch. 7): A name used univocally said of many things which differ only as individuals, but are of the same kind; or a name signifying a particular kind of thing within a genus.

Difference (ch. 7): A name used univocally, said of many things, signifying how they are what they are.

Property (ch. 7): A name used univocally which signifies something necessarily following from what a thing is.

Accident (ch. 7): A being which exists in another, not through itself. (accident vs. substance) A name used univocally which signifies that which happens to belong to a thing, but does not follow from what the thing is. (accident vs. property)

Definition (ch. 7): Speech signifying distinctly what a thing is.

Name (ch. 7): Speech having no part which signifies by itself.

Statement (ch. 8): Speech signifying the true or the false.

Reasoning (ch. 6): Coming to know or guess a statement from other statements and because of them.

Argument (ch. 6): Speech bringing together the statements from which we reason.

Example (ch. 9): An argument from one singular to another singular of the same kind.

Induction (ch. 10): An argument which leads from many particulars to a universal.

Enthymeme (ch. 9): An argument from likelihood or signs.

Syllogism (ch. 9): Speech in which some statements having been set down another statement follows necessarily because of them.

Demonstration (ch. 10): A syllogism causing someone to know a conclusion perfectly.

Reason (ch. 3): The part of man's soul which allows him to understand what is true or false.

Will (ch. 3): The part of man's soul which allows him to choose what is good or evil.

Form (ch. 7): That cause which makes a thing to be what it is.

Chapter 1

Chapter 1 is a very brief history of the beginnings of philosophy. It begins with an explanation of what conditions were necessary before philosophy could begin and what motivated the first philosophers.

Questions about Chapter 1

Why was some kind of leisure necessary as a condition before philosophy could begin in earnest?

Why is wonder at the beginning of philosophy?

What is the difference between poetic myth and philosophy?

What group is widely regarded as the first true philosophers? What were they seeking in their philosophy?

Were the early philosophers all in fundamental disagreement, or were there some areas of fundamental agreement?

Is a history of philosophy and philosophers the same thing as doing philosophy?

What is the reason for examining the teachings of a few of the early philosophers in a brief history of philosophy before defining philosophy?

Chapter 2

Chapter 2 formulates a definition of philosophy: an account (that is, a setting in order) of the ultimate causes of reality according to reason. In light of that definition, the chapter addresses some objections to and misconceptions about philosophy.

Questions about Chapter 2

What is the difference between philosophy and science (especially the so-called experimental sciences)? Is there some sense in which philosophy can also be called a science?

Answer this objection: Philosophers always disagree while scientists always agree, therefore, philosophy cannot be a science or arrive at certain truth.

Answer this objection: Philosophy is based upon each person's experience, but each person's experience is merely subjective. Therefore, philosophy is merely subjective.

What are some reasons why we should expect more disagreement among philosophers than among scientists?

Is it possible to arrive at certain truth through philosophy?

Given the definition of philosophy, is mathematics somehow included as a part of philosophy?

What is the difference between philosophy and theology?

Given that philosophy involves setting ultimate causes in order, where would one expect to find philosophers disagreeing?

Given the definition of philosophy, can anyone with the use of reason really live without philosophizing?

Chapter 3

Chapter 3 gives an overview of all the branches of knowledge and shows their mutual relationships to each other. More particularly, it gives the divisions of the various branches of knowledge and explains why each branch is distinct from the others. This prepares the student to see how the various disciplines he will study this year (logic, natural philosophy, ethics) are related to one another.

Questions about Chapter 3

Given the definition of philosophy, why should it belong to philosophy to give a universal roadmap to all things knowable? For example, why shouldn't the mathematician or the chemist consider the whole body of knowledge?

Why is it that everything that can be known has some order? What is the relation of this order to philosophy? (Hint: consider the definition of philosophy.)

What two things are necessary for something to be known?

What are the three types of order with respect to reason?

What makes a speculative science different from a practical science? That is, what is the end (or purpose) of each?

Rather than an insult, why is it a compliment to say that speculative science is "useless"?

Which kind of knowledge is better: speculative or practical? Why? Which one does logic primarily aim at?

What are the divisions of the speculative sciences?

What are the types of the practical sciences?

Does speculative science depend upon practical science, or is it the other way around?

Where on this map would sciences like physics, biology, and chemistry fall?

Where would arts like carpentry and painting fall?

What does logic order in man? What does ethics order in man?

Chapter 4

CHAPTER 4 GIVES THE DEFINITION of logic and explains the relationship of logic to the other arts. It also explains what kind of knowledge logic helps us to acquire. Finally, this chapter explains why some statements are known through themselves (as opposed to being known through an argument).

Questions about Chapter 4

What is art?

Why are there two definitions of logic? How are they different?

Why is logic called the "art of arts"?

Why is art proper to rational beings? Why doesn't the fact that animals build things like nests and webs mean that they also have some kind of art?

What are the two types of knowledge? Of these two types of knowledge, which one does logic strengthen?

If logic puts order into the acts of reason, what does this imply about when logic should be studied? For example, should logic be studied at the beginning, in the middle, or at the end of philosophy?

How do we reason; that is, what do we reason from and what do we reason to? What are their names?

Must all truths be proven by an argument? Why or why not?

What are "self-evident truths"? Why must they exist?

Chapter 5

CHAPTER 5 CONSIDERS WHETHER LOGIC is really necessary, or if it is even possible. These questions must be addressed before beginning logic since, if logic is unnecessary, it will be useless to study it, and if logic is impossible, it will be a waste of time to study it. First, the chapter raises some difficulties to the need for logic (for example, the fact that most people can live their lives well without it). The text then answers these difficulties. Next, the text gives two objections why logic seems impossible.

Questions about Chapter 5

Is logic necessary to know everything? For example, it is necessary to sense colors, or to know that 1+1 = 2?

Is logic necessary to be a good painter or sculptor?

Is logic possible? How?

Other than the fallacy of equivocation, what are some other common kinds of mistakes that people often make when reasoning about difficult matters?

Answers to Questions in Chapter 5

The text also provides two questions for which it does not give answers. I will provide a brief answer to these two questions here. The two questions are:

What is the difficulty Socrates presents in the *Meno* with trying to discover something which you do not know? What is the solution to this difficulty?

The difficulty of Socrates in the *Meno* can be summed up in the following argument:

Either (a) you come to know what you already know or (b) you come to know what you do not know. But you cannot come to know what you already know any more than you can come to own what you already own. So (a) seems false. And you cannot come to know what you in no way know, since if you did, you would be getting something from nothing. So (b) seems false. Therefore, since (a) and (b) seem to be the only two options for coming to know, and both are impossible, it seems that it is impossible to come to know anything.

The answer is that there is a middle ground between knowing actually and not knowing in any way. This middle ground is knowing potentially. Take a simple example: We say that if you know the sides of a rectangle, you know its area. But what we really mean is that if you actually know the sides of a rectangle, you are *able to* know its area (this becomes clear if the numbers expressing the length for each side of the rectangle are very large numbers). So between options (a) and (b), there is a third option: (c) you come to actually know from what you potentially know.

Chapter 6

CHAPTER 6 LAYS THE GROUNDWORK for dividing up logic into its three parts: the art of defining, the art about statements, and the art of reasoning. These three parts of logic correspond to the three acts of reason which they direct: understanding what a thing is, understanding the true and the false, and reasoning. The acts of reason are not directly sensed by us. Instead, we look at human speech to distinguish the three acts of reason. Speech is the immediate subject matter of logic, just as wood is the subject matter of carpentry. The carpenter works directly on the wood, and the logician works directly upon our speech. Only by putting order into our speech can the logician put order into the corresponding acts of reason.

Next, chapter 6 works backwards from the good which logic aims at to the tools needed to obtain this good. Just as a carpenter aims at the good of furniture and reasons backwards to the tools he needs to shape wood, like a saw and a hammer and nails, so too the logician aims at true and necessary conclusions and then reasons backwards to the tools he needs to arrive at that conclusion. First, he sees that he needs arguments that are able to arrive at true and necessary conclusions. Then, since arguments are composed of statements (called premises), he reasons that statements are necessary tools of logic. Finally, since statements are composed of terms, he reasons that he needs definition as a tool to understand the meaning of the terms. From this we can see that the first part of logic is the art of defining, the second part of logic is the art about statements, and the third part of logic is the art about arguments or syllogizing.

Questions about Chapter 6

What are words?

____

____

____

Why do we come to understand the three acts of reason through the three kinds of speech (names, statements, and arguments)?

____

____

____

Why is our speech better known than our thoughts?

What is a demonstration?

What is a demonstration composed of?

Why is the art of defining the first art we must learn in logic? Why is the art of syllogizing the last thing we learn in logic?

Chapter 7

Chapter 7 considers the art of defining. This is the first part of logic, and this chapter is quite long compared to the previous chapters. Defining is the foundation of all logic, so take your time in reading and understanding this chapter. The chapter is divided into two parts.

The first part considers names, including the kinds of names which are used to construct definitions (univocal names). Every definition starts with a univocal name. If your name is used equivocally, you have to reduce it to a single meaning before you begin defining. For example, if you want to define the name "gold," you have to decide whether you are defining the substance gold or the color gold (which is a kind of quality).

The second part considers definition, beginning under the heading "kinds of definition." This second part takes up the majority of the chapter.

The ultimate purpose of this chapter is to teach the student to construct definitions. Therefore, practice making definitions is essential to achieve the aim of this chapter. First, you need to decide what kind of definition you are making. Nominal definitions are the easiest to make. The next easiest are definitions by properties. Essential definitions are the hardest to make, and sometimes it is not possible to make one. For example, it is not possible to make an essential definition of a bee or a rose. A definition begins with the genus so that is the first part of the definition for which you should hunt. The ten categories are the highest genera, so normally you will begin a definition of a name by determining which category it falls under. The properties given for each category are especially helpful in this regard. For example, a property of quality is that qualities are said to be similar or dissimilar. Right away we can see how that helps us with a word like "culture." One culture is said to be similar or dissimilar to another, so that tells us that the name "culture" is under the category of quality.

After finding your category, the next step is to use the additional tools given in this chapter to divide your genus so you can approach a more specific definition. The sections on opposites, before and after, etc., can help greatly with this process. The following is a list of tools you can use in order to construct a good definition of a given name:

Definition Toolbox

1. Is your name used univocally or equivocally? You can distinguish the meanings of words by seeing if it has different contraries (for example, the contrary of dry is both wet and sweet, which shows that dry has two meanings). You can also place the name together with a term it modifies to distinguish its meanings (for example, sharp has many meanings, as in a sharp knife, sharp cheese, and a sharp note).

2. Are you giving a nominal definition, a definition by properties, or an essential definition?

3. Are you defining a complete or incomplete thing?

4. Are you defining a natural or artificial thing?

5. What category are you in? Here you should make use of the marks or properties for each category, especially the most proper mark. For example, it is most proper to quantities that they are said to be equal or unequal, and to qualities that they are said to be similar or dissimilar.

6. Does the thing named reduce back to a category as something imperfect?

7. Use the three roads to definition.

8. If approaching from more universal terms, divide the genus using opposites.

9. If giving an essential definition, is your difference how it is what it is?

10. Use before and after to order your differences.

11. Check using the four marks of a good definition.

12. Remember that there are four possible kinds of causes; an essential definition should include at least the formal cause.

Questions about Chapter 7

Why is the genus the beginning of every definition?

How do we know that there are many highest genera instead of just one (like "being")?

What signs indicate that each of the ten categories are beings in a different (equivocal) sense of the word?

What signs indicate that there are no other categories besides the ten listed by Aristotle? Consider especially evidence that there is nothing left out in between categories or on either end (before substance or after outfit).

What should we do if a name does not fit naturally into one category (like motion)?

Why does logic teach us how to begin definitions but doesn't always teach us how to complete every definition?

What are the four causes?

Sample Exercise

This sample exercise is an example of how to go about defining names using the tools provided in chapter 7.

Sample: Defining "health."

1. Distinguish the primary meanings of health: bodily health vs. mental health. Here I am defining bodily or physical health as can be found in any animal.

2. What kind of definition is this? It is an essential definition (a definition giving the causes of health).

3. Health is something incomplete (it is an accident in a substance). Therefore, I will have to include its proper subject in the definition. This subject is an animal body.

4. Health is natural, so it should fall into a single category.

5. What category is health in? Looking at the marks, it seems to be a quality since it has a contrary (sickness), it allows of more or less, and it is similar to things (for example, health is similar to sanity: health is to the body what sanity is to the mind).

6. Health fits in the category of quality and doesn't need to be reduced back to it.

7. What species of quality is health? Health is a disposition (first species of quality).

8. Can we make further divisions into species? Yes. We can approach this definition from above—that is, by dividing the genus into species.

9. Our differences should be essential differences, indicating *how* a disposition of an animal body is *what it is*. Health is obviously a good disposition, as opposed to sickness which is a bad disposition. And since health is a good disposition of an animal body and the essence of being an animal involves life and sensation, health will be the kind of disposition which causes perfect life and sensation. This happens when the essential elements of an animal body are rightly disposed to produce optimum sensation and living activities.

10. So we can now state our provisional definition of health as a quality, and more specifically a disposition, of the essential elements of an animal body which is such as to produce optimal sensation and living activities.

11. This definition seems to satisfy the four marks of a good essential definition.

12. Of the four causes, this definition of health includes the formal cause (disposition), the material cause (elements of an animal body), and the final cause (to produce optimal sensation and living activities).

    Of course, there may be more specific causes which a doctor may be able to identify which could enter into the definition of health. The logician does not necessarily have all of the requisite experiences to make a complete definition of health in terms of all of its proper causes. For example, the logician would not know the proper agent cause or causes of health, nor would he know the exact nature of the essential elements of an animal body. Nevertheless, the definition we have provided is a good beginning, and it is left to the more particular art of medicine to complete the definition.

Chapter 8

Chapter 8 teaches the art about statements. The first part of this chapter gives a definition of statement and explains this definition. The next part of this chapter gives and explains various possible divisions of statements (for example, affirmative/negative, universal/particular, simple/compound, modal/non-modal). In dividing the various kinds of statements, this chapter also indicates the relationships which exist among some of these kinds of statements (for example, the universal affirmative statement is related to the particular negative statement as its contradictory and to the universal negative statement as its contrary). The conclusion of this chapter explains self-evident and *per se* statements which, as we shall later see, are the building blocks of the ultimate tool of logic: the demonstration.

Questions about Chapter 8

What is a statement?

Is a statement one thing or many things?

Why are statements more closely connected with things (reality) than definitions?

The chapter gives many divisions of statement. Which division is a division of the genus "statement" into its species? Why?

Are all of the kinds of statements mentioned in this chapter called "statement" univocally? If not, which kinds of statements are called statements in the proper and primary sense?

How does understanding definition help one to determine if a statement is self-evident?

How does understanding definition help one to determine if a statement is *per se* (in any of the three senses of *per se*)?

Examples of *Per Se* Premises

Per se premises are the necessary ingredients for a perfect argument. In order to give the student a broader range of experience with *per se* statements, I have included the following list of examples for each of the three kinds of *per se* statements.

Per se 1: The predicate is in the definition of the subject

Man is an animal.
A crow is a bird.
Double is a relation.
Five is a quantity.
Round is a shape.
Patience is a virtue.
Heat is a quality.
A bachelor is unmarried.

Per se 2: The subject is in the definition of the predicate (definition of incomplete thing)

A number is either even or odd.
A line is either curved or straight.
A body is either in motion or at rest.
A surface is colored.
A nose is snub.
A substance has accidents.
A figure has shape.
A living body is ensouled.

Per se 3: The predicate belongs to the subject as to its immediate cause

The swimming man is wet.
The slaughtered animal dies.
A body is united with its shape.
A living body is united with its soul.
A whole is greater than its part.
Motion is in a definite direction.
A body moves another body by contact.
A sphere casts a circular shadow.
Mind produces order.
Creatures are created.
The perfection of a thing is its good.

Nature exists.
Substance causes accidents.
Substance exists.
Many kinds of substances exist.
Animal exists.
Man exists.

Chapter 9

CHAPTER 9 CONSIDERS ARGUMENTS, AND more specifically, the argument called a syllogism. This chapter considers the form of the argument, while the next chapter will consider syllogisms from the perspective of their matter. The first part of the chapter considers the definition of syllogism and reasons from this definition to some properties that belong to every syllogism (for example, to the fact that every syllogism must have a middle term). The second part considers the simple syllogism, and the third part considers the if-then and either-or syllogisms.

Much of the chapter is dedicated to giving the reasons why some forms of syllogism are valid, while other forms are not. Once the student understands these reasons, however, the aim is to give the student a practical method of determining whether any given syllogism is valid or not. To this end, the rules for determining the validity of a syllogism (for example, the rule that no valid syllogism results from two negative premises and the SUN PIN rule) should be practiced frequently.

The following is an example of how to evaluate a syllogism using these rules.

All men are able to identify their grandparents.
No dolphins are able to identify their grandparents.

Step 1: Is there a univocal middle term? Yes, "able to identify their grandparents" is the middle term, and it is used in the same sense in both premises.

Step 2: What figure is this syllogism? Second figure, since the middle term is in the predicate of both premises.

Step 3: Are there two negative premises? No.

Step 4: Are there two particular premises? No.

Step 5: Is the middle term distributed (SUN PIN rule)? Yes, since "able to identify their grandparents" is the predicate in the negative premise.

Step 6: Does the A-O exception apply (the Harry Belafonte rule)? No, since this is not first figure nor is there an O (particular negative) premise.

Step 7: Now that we know that something follows from these premises in this form, what is the strongest conclusion we can have? The strongest conclusion we can have is a universal negative (E) statement, since both premises are universal but one premise is negative.

Step 8: Now that we know we can get a universal negative conclusion, which term is the minor term and which is the major term in the conclusion? In this case, it doesn't matter, because every E statement is convertible: "No men are dolphins" converts to "No dolphins are men." But for the sake of consistency, we normally place the major premise on top, so that would imply that "men" is the major term. Thus, we can conclude "No dolphins are men."

The student should practice using these rules until he can evaluate any syllogism within a matter of a few seconds. It might even be helpful to time him as he evaluates a syllogism. In order to show mastery of the subject, it should take a student less than five seconds to determine if a syllogism is valid (steps 1-6 above) and less than thirty seconds to determine exactly what conclusion follows in a valid syllogism (steps 1-8 above).

The student should also be able to evaluate the forms of the if-then and either-or syllogisms. These forms are simpler and easier to evaluate than the forms of the simple syllogism.

Questions about Chapter 9

How do the various relationships among kinds of statements explained in chapter 8 help us to evaluate whether or not a syllogism is valid?

____

____

____

What three things are needed to form a syllogism?

____

____

____

What are the definitions of middle term, major term, minor term, major premise, and minor premise?

____

____

____

What makes one term to be "major" and the other to be "minor"?

____

____

____

____

What does it mean to say that a term is distributed?

Why is the first figure better known to us?

How does the conversion of statements explained in the previous chapter statements help us to evaluate if a syllogism is valid or not?

Are the terms in a simple syllogism called "terms" in the same sense as the terms in if-then or either-or syllogisms?

Chapter 10

CHAPTER 10 CONSIDERS THE MOST perfect form of argument: the demonstration. The art of demonstration brings together all of the other parts of logic, and the tool of demonstration is a composite tool which includes the tools of definition, statement, and syllogism. It should be noted that while demonstration is the most perfect form of argument, it is not always possible to construct a demonstration about every subject matter. Some matters, such as moral choices, the actions of individual, material substances, etc., do not allow of the kind of necessity and certitude required for a demonstration. Therefore, demonstrative knowledge should not be demanded or even sought in every argument, as not every matter *can* give demonstrative knowledge. Sometimes probable knowledge is the best that can be achieved. Nevertheless, it is helpful even in these cases to see what perfect knowledge would look like and to somehow approximate demonstrated knowledge as much as possible.

Chapter 10 begins with a definition of demonstration, followed by an explanation of the definition. Next, the chapter uses this definition to show what kinds of materials should be sought and assembled in order to form a demonstration. Premises of a demonstration must have six attributes, all of which are found in self-evident and *per se* premises discussed in chapter 8.

Next, the chapter treats of the different kinds of demonstration (cause to effect, effect to cause, etc.). Common to all of these kinds of demonstration is the fact that the conclusions of these arguments are necessary, certain, and true. Distinguishing between cause to effect and effect to cause arguments exercises the student's natural ability to distinguish causes from their *per se* and proper effects and to recognize the order between them.

The chapter concludes with a treatment of the ways in which names can be used equivocally and an investigation into the process of induction. These two topics are necessary to understand how someone might come to know a conclusion through an analogous middle term and how it is possible arrive at certain, necessary, and self-evident premises by way of induction.

Questions about Chapter 10

What are the three reasons for why demonstrations are better than probable arguments?

What are the six qualities which every premise of a demonstration must have?

How can one argue from the end (final cause) of a demonstration to the form and matter of a demonstration?

How do the arts about definition, statement, and syllogism each contribute to the art about demonstration?

Are proper quid, quia 1, and quia 2 demonstrations all called demonstrations univocally? Put another way, is demonstration a genus with these three kinds of demonstration as its species?

What is certitude? Based upon your answer, show why some kinds of knowledge are more certain than others.

If a name is used equivocally by reason, how could it possibly serve as a middle term to produce certain knowledge?

Some inductions terminate in a certain conclusion, while others do not. Is this because they use a different form of argument or because of some other cause?

What is the difference between intuition and induction?

Is the act of intuition natural or artificial?

Final Essay Question

Suppose that you are writing to someone who sees no reason why anyone should study logic. Beginning with the good at which logic aims, show that this good is very desirable and that logic, in all of its major parts, is necessary to obtain that good.

Explain the relation of logic to the other sciences. Defend the fact that logic is a practical rather than a speculative science. What are some problems that would result in the art of logic itself if someone studied logic for its own sake (similar to the way mathematics is studied)?